THE POWER OF RESET

Inspirational Quotes to Change Your Life

DENISE CUTRONE

Copyright © 2025 (Denise Cutrone)
All rights reserved worldwide.

No part of the book may be copied or changed in any format, sold, or used in a way other than what is outlined in this book, under any circumstances, without the prior written permission of the publisher.

Inspiring Publishers
P.O. Box 159, Calwell, ACT Australia 2905
Email: publishaspg@gmail.com
http://www.inspiringpublishers.com

A catalogue record for this book is available from the National Library of Australia

National Library of Australia The Prepublication Data Service

Author: Denise Cutrone
Title: The Power of Reset
Genre: Non-fiction, Inspirational

Paperback ISBN: 978-1-923250-78-9
ePub2 ISBN: 978-1-923250-79-6

Table of Contents

Introduction v
Reset 1
Change 13
Master Your Vibration 35
Create Your Reality 59
Overthinking 80
Be Yourself 97
Practice Gratitude 105
Love Is the Answer 112
In Closing 122

Introduction

We are all spiritual beings living a human experience so we are energy, not form. Our bodies are form, but they are only a vehicle to carry us through this physical experience.

When we die, our physical body dies but our soul lives on. We leave our body and join all who have left us in the multidimensional world of spirit.

With every ending, there is a new beginning. Keep your heart open and know that everything you are experiencing is happening for you, not too you.

We have the power to reset and re-create our lives at any moment. At any moment you can turn the page and start creating a new story.

We all have a gift, find yours and share it with the world.

*Dedicated to my beautiful mother Carmelina,
a woman of strength, kindness, and unconditional love.
You will live in my heart forever.*

*With the flick of a thought,
you can change the direction of your life.*

Reset

*No matter where you are in life,
you can press the reset button at any moment and
change it, it all starts from the inside out.*

To reset and recreate, we must align with our energetic vibration and become what we desire.

Change your perception.

We create from the inside out.

Everything we need to access is not out there,
it is within us.

Feel good as this will raise your vibration and make you a magnet for manifesting.

Open your mind and dream big, don't live small.

Don't judge what you don't understand.

Begin with loving yourself.

Fill your own gaps, so that you bring the best version of yourself to any relationship.

Show up as your true authentic self,
whatever that looks like.

Reset and re-invent yourself.

Change

Creating change from the inside out

During change we grow.

Bless your past and all the people
who played a role in it so that you can move
forward into a new direction.

Embrace change, let it help you grow.

Change your perception, it will change your life.

Focus on what you want,
not on what you don't want.

Ask yourself;

- Am I happy?
- If not, how did I end up here?
- What have I identified as a familiar pattern?
- What do I want to change?
- What will I do to change it?

Get clear on what you want and take action.

Don't let fear and anxiety stop you
from moving forward.

Taking the first step to change is rewarding.
You are telling the universe that you are ready
and things around you will begin to shift
in the direction of your desires.

Ask yourself;

- What do I want?
- What do I need to do in order to take a step in that direction?
- Do it.

Life will never be perfect.
We will always face challenges, but how we deal with our challenges is where our power lies.

Embrace change.

When things get tough, don't give up.
Keep going.

Every challenge prepares you
for what lies ahead.
Trust the journey.

If it feels good, go with it.
If it doesn't feel good, let it go.

Listen to your intuition.

Focus on your breath, this is the quickest way back to alignment.

Forgive yourself and others.

Forgiveness liberates you.

How people treat you is a reflection of themselves, not you.

Good things start to happen when you send out joy and good vibes.

Master Your Vibration

When we master our vibration, we master our life.

To master your life, you will need to master your vibration.

When you learn to master your vibration
and direct your thoughts to what you want
instead of what you don't want, everything you
need will come to you at the right time.

Let go of whatever is not working so that you come into vibrational alignment.

As you clear out the old you make room
for the new.

Chaos is just fear that is created
by you in your mind as you
enter unfamiliar territory, the unknown.

Don't cling to the known.

Life is all about change, and as we grow and evolve so too does our circle.

Choose your circle wisely,
you become the company
you surround yourself with.

Doors will close, but others will open.

As we take new paths,
we must say goodbye to old stories.

When you are clear on what you want,
doors will open for you.

We are energy, so the energy you send out through your thoughts, your attitude, and your vibration is what you will attract back to you.

What you give energy to is what will expand in your life.

We control our thoughts and actions,
focus only on what you want and let the rest go.

Meditation is one of the quickest ways to raise
your vibration and align your energy.
It strengthens the mind and creates inner peace.

Peace starts from within.

Our outer world is a reflection
of our inner world.

In silence you will hear the answers you seek
as you connect to your true source.

Whatever brings you peace and tranquility
is your meditation practice.
As you practice your meditation,
focus on your breath, as this will help you
become fully present.

You will attract into your life whatever you
focus on, so focus only on
what you want not on what you don't want.

Imagine you are a magnet
and your energy is magnetic.
What you put out there is what you
will attract back to you.

You are the director of your life,
only you can make your next move.

Feel good as much as you can,
as this will raise your vibration
and draw to you your desires.

Create Your Reality

Ask yourself why you want what you want, this will help you bring in what is meant for you.

Every decision you make creates your life.

We are energy, and we create
with our thoughts and feelings.

What you tune into, is what you will
bring into your frequency.

Whatever you focus on grows,
so focus only on what you want,
not on what you don't want.

If you catch yourself thinking about what you don't want, stop, release, and align yourself with the present moment.

Don't settle and don't ignore red flags.

Don't underestimate your strength and courage.

Love yourself so that you can be the
best version of yourself.

Open your heart and leave the past behind you.

Everyone you meet helps you get closer
to who you truly are.

Bless your past with love.

The strength within you is much stronger
than any obstacle.

Don't fill your void with addictions,
as the void will only get bigger.

Stay present, in the moment as often as you can as this will open up the right pathway for you.

The answers we seek are within us.

Spiritual immunity builds mental strength.

Switch off from the world and
be in the moment.

Follow your passions and let them guide you to your purpose in life.

There are no limits to what you can create in your life.

You are the creator.

Find your gift, and share it with the world.

Overthinking

The art to destroying your life.

Stop thinking and just be.

Accept this moment for what it is.

Breathe and focus on your breath.
It is the quickest way to align yourself.

We struggle when we go against what is.

Let go of how you think it should be
and just be.

Accept the moment for what it is.
This will help you surrender.

Trust in the process of life.

Be clear on what you want and let the rest go.

Relax and surrender, have faith that
there is a higher force at work
that will always work with you,
for your highest good.

Walk in confidence, knowing that you are right where you need to be.

Accept rejection, as this is often Gods
way of protecting you
from something you can't yet see for yourself.

This moment is preparing you
for what's up ahead.

Keep life simple and take in the moment,
make each moment count.

Everyone you meet plays a role in your life
and you play a role in theirs.

Practice non-judgment, always.

Everything you need will come to you.
All you need to do is focus on what you want.

Be Yourself

*Being your true authentic self is the most powerful gift
you can give to yourself and to others.*

All experiences help us grow.

Be your true authentic self, always.

We all have a different path,
so don't compare yourself to others.

Being honest with yourself is the only path to happiness and freedom.

The best revenge is no revenge,
move on with love in your heart.

Surround yourself with people
who want to see you succeed.

Walk your talk and always be true
to who you are.

Practice Gratitude

Gratitude is the road to abundance.

Focus on feeling good, the better you feel the higher your vibration becomes, which makes you a magnet to abundance.

Happiness is a feeling, and this feeling comes from within. It stems from love, and it continues to grow when we begin to appreciate the small things in life.

Be grateful for all the daily things you take for granted.

Start your day in gratitude.

Appreciate everything and everyone in your life as they are a blessing.

Thank God for your blessings.

Love Is the Answer

Love conquers all.

Love helps people become the best version of themselves.

Love and accept people for who they are.

Face your challenges and use them
as an opportunity to strengthen yourself
in ways that will develop you.

If you are filled with love and kindness, you will attract love and kindness wherever you go.

Send out love and you will receive love.

When you come from a place of love,
you will always feel safe,
as love is who you are.

Loving yourself is the most precious
gift you will ever give to
yourself and to others.

Allow what comes, it will come, and it will pass.

You are love, and you are loved unconditionally.

In Closing

Everyone who enters your life does so for a reason, and it will reveal itself to you as you continue on your path.

You are a gift. God created you to be you, and by being you, you will touch many lives in different ways.

Choose love over fear, always.

Be loving and kind and lift people up whenever you can. A small act of kindness toward someone could change their direction completely.

Love is always the answer. It fills that empty space and transforms people. When you open your heart to love, you open the door to happiness and abundance.

Much love

www.ingramcontent.com/pod-product-compliance
Lightning Source LLC
Chambersburg PA
CBHW041145110526
44590CB00027B/4126